# PAINTING ROCKS

By Dana Meachen Rau • Illustrated by Kathleen Petelinsek

CHERRY LAKE PUBLISHING • ANN ARBOR, MICHIGAN

CHERRY
LAKE
Publishing

Published in the United States of America by Cherry Lake Publishing
Ann Arbor, Michigan
www.cherrylakepublishing.com

Content Adviser: Dr. Julia L. Hovanec, Professor of Art Education, Kutztown University, Kutztown, Pennsylvania

Photo Credits: Page 4, ©Delphid/Dreamstime.com; page 6, ©Cristian Tzecu/Dreamstime.com; page 7, ©Pichugin Dmitry/Shutterstock, Inc.; pages 25, 26, and 27, Dana Meachen Rau; page 32, Tania McNaboe

Library of Congress Cataloging-in-Publication Data
Rau, Dana Meachen, 1971–
  Painting rocks / by Dana Meachen Rau.
    pages cm — (How-to library. Crafts)
  Includes bibliographical references and index.
  ISBN 978-1-61080-479-0 (lib. bdg.) —
ISBN 978-1-61080-566-7 (e-book) — ISBN 978-1-61080-653-4 (pbk.)
1. Stone painting—Juvenile literature. 2. Acrylic painting—Juvenile literature. I. Title.
  TT370.R38 2012
  751.42'6—dc23                                  2012002128

Cherry Lake Publishing would like to acknowledge the work of The Partnership for 21st Century Skills. Please visit www.21stcenturyskills.org for more information.

Printed in the United States of America
Corporate Graphics Inc.
July 2012
CLFA11

HOW-TO LIBRARY

# TABLE OF CONTENTS

# Observe the World

No two rocks are exactly the same!

Everyone looks at the world in his or her own way. When you go for a walk, what do you notice? Tall buildings? Fields of flowers? Bright sunsets? Mighty mountains?

Next time you're out for a walk, look under your feet! Lots of people collect rocks. They might add them to a collection at home. Or maybe they save them for another hobby—like rock painting.

Rock painting is a fun way to make a plain rock into something special. A flat smooth rock is best for painting. It is like a tiny **canvas**. You can paint anything you can imagine. The best places to find flat smooth rocks are near an ocean or along a river. If you can't find smooth rocks, look for ones with interesting shapes, bumps, and points. Maybe you'll find one that is shaped like a heart or a nose. Let the rock help you decide what to paint.

Choose the right rocks for your project.

SMOOTH MOVES

Rocks are solid and don't seem to change. But rocks **erode** over time. This wears them down and changes their shape. Water is one of the natural forces that change rocks. A running river or ocean waves move over rocks and smooth out their rough edges. That's why smooth rocks are found near bodies of water.

# On the Walls

You never know what you might find in a cave.

Caves can be mysterious. These large, rocky underground spaces can have lots of passageways. People wear headlamps and other special gear to explore them. People have made some amazing discoveries, including ancient paintings on rock walls.

The earliest cave painters lived in the Stone Age. The Stone Age is the name given to a time period long ago when people used stone tools to hunt and gather their food. The oldest cave paintings are more than 30,000 years old.

These artists used **minerals** from the soil to make their paint. They painted with their hands, with brushes made from animal hair, or with other natural tools. They created pictures of animals, such as lions, mammoths, and horses.

Historians trace the beginnings of art to the cave paintings of the Stone Age. You can continue this art form today by painting on rocks.

Cave paintings have helped us learn about the lives of ancient people.

# Basic Tools

The supplies you need to paint rocks are similar to supplies you would need for any sort of painting project.

## Tools to Keep Things Clean
- *Newspaper or vinyl tablecloth*—to cover your workspace
- *Apron or smock*—to cover your clothes
- *Small container of water*—to clean your brushes
- *Paper towels*—to dry your brushes
- *Scrub brush, old toothbrush, and cooling rack*—to clean and dry your rocks
- *Felt circles*—to place under your rock to protect furniture from scratches

## Tools for Drawing and Painting
- *Sketch paper or tracing paper*—to plan your design
- *Pencils and chalk*—to draw images onto your rock
- *Acrylic paint*—to paint your rock; comes in tubes and bottles in lots of colors, dries quickly, and covers rocks well
- *Brushes*—for painting; come in many sizes and shapes; flat brushes are good for large areas, round brushes for smaller areas, and liner brushes for details
- *Palette or coated paper plate*—to hold and mix paint
- *Permanent markers*—to add fine details after the paint has dried
- *Varnish*—to seal your rock

## CLEANING BRUSHES

Don't let acrylic paint dry on your brushes. They will become stiff and unusable. To clean off your brush, swirl it in a container of water, take it out, and gently squeeze the bristles between paper towels. When you are done painting for the day, rinse the brushes well in the sink. Use soap to make sure they are completely clean and set them upright in a container to dry.

## COLOR WHEEL

Paint comes in lots of colors. But you can make a rainbow with just three colors: red, yellow, and blue.

Red + blue = purple

Blue + yellow = green

Yellow + red = orange

Lighten colors by adding white. This is called a tint. Darken them by adding a little bit of black. This is called a shade.

9

# Preparing the Rock

Always clean your rocks before you paint them.

If you found your rocks near a river or at the beach, they may already be clean. But if you found them in the woods, in a park, or at the side of a road, they may still be dirty. Paint sticks best to a clean rock. So it is important to clean your rocks well before getting started.

Run your rock under warm water in the sink. Rub it with a scrub brush. Use an old toothbrush to get in the cracks. Pat the rock dry with paper towels. Then place it on a cooling rack so air can get to it on all sides. It will take about 30 to 60 minutes for your rock to dry, depending on the **humidity** of the air. If it is a sunny day, put your rock outside to dry.

If your rock is a dark color, you may want to paint a base **coat**. A base coat is a thin layer of white paint that will help brighten the colors you paint on top of it.

CHECK FIRST
Before you collect a rock, make sure it's okay to take it! Don't take rocks from someone's garden or stone wall. Nature preserves do not allow you to take rocks either.

**To paint a base coat:**

1. Squeeze some white paint onto your palette. Dip a flat brush into the paint.
2. Paint the top and sides of your rock, covering it well. Try to paint with brushstrokes all in the same direction.
3. Set the rock aside to dry. Drying can take about 15 minutes to an hour, depending on the thickness of the paint and the humidity of the air. Clean the brush right away and set it aside to dry, too.
4. You don't have to paint the bottom of your rock, since no one will see it. But if you want to, wait for the top and sides to dry, flip it over, and paint the bottom.

A white base coat will make your other colors brighter.

# Drawing

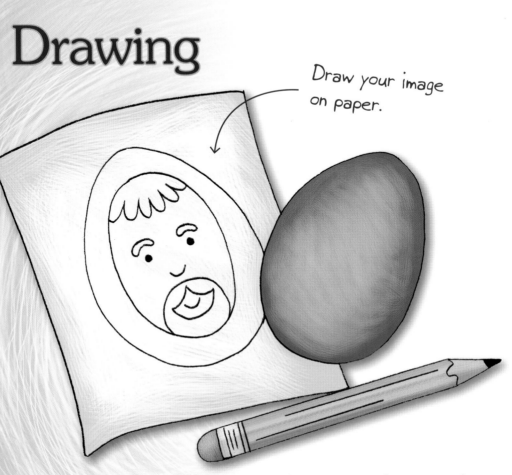

Draw your image on paper.

Sketch out some ideas on paper. When you are happy with your image, you can draw it right onto the rock with a sharp pencil.

You can also **transfer** an image from your paper to the rock. Here's how:

1. Trace your rock onto a piece of paper or tracing paper. Draw your image within the outline on the paper.
2. Flip the paper over. Scribble over the back until all the lines of your image are covered with pencil (if the rock is a light color) or chalk (if the rock is dark).

Scribble over the back of the image and retrace your lines to transfer it onto your rock.

3. Turn the paper back to the front side and place it on the rock. Hold it still or tape it down so it doesn't move while you trace. Retrace the lines of the original image on the paper, pressing hard with the pencil.

4. Remove the paper. Your image will be transferred onto your rock.

You can transfer words onto your rock, too. Write out words by hand or print them out from the computer in a **font** you like. Transfer them the same way as described above.

Keep your sketch handy. As you paint areas of your rock, you will probably cover some of your pencil lines. You may have to transfer the image again onto a painted area.

### SIT STILL

Before you start drawing, place your rock on a flat surface. Figure out the best way for it to sit without wobbling or falling over. This will help you choose the best side to draw your image on.

# Painting

Use a palette or paper plate to hold your paint.

Paint your image in stages to allow time for the paint to dry between colors. If you try to paint one color on top of or next to another color while the paints are still wet, the colors will blend and get muddy.

1. Squeeze a little bit of the color you need onto your palette. If you squeeze out too much, the paint might start to harden before you are done working with it. You can always add more.

2. Paint the background first. A flat brush is best to cover large areas. Pick up a little paint at a time. If it's too thick, dab the brush on the palette or a paper towel to remove the extra paint.

3. Rinse your brush. Set the rock aside to dry.
4. If the first color isn't dark enough, give it another coat. Let it dry again.
5. Continue painting other areas of the image with a round brush, letting the paint dry between colors. Be sure to constantly rinse your brush so the paint doesn't harden on it.

## PAINTING TECHNIQUES

- If you want your colors to blend together, don't let them dry. Mix and swirl them right on the rock.
- Spread out the hairs of a dry brush and dip the tips in paint. Then gently brush it against your rock to make a furry effect. This is called the dry brush technique.
- You don't even have to use a paintbrush. Try dabbing paint onto your rock with a sponge, cotton swab, or toothbrush.

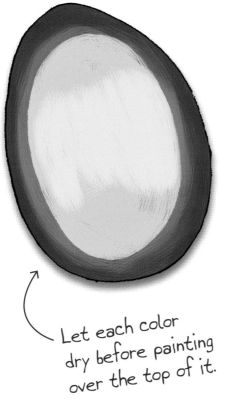

Let each color dry before painting over the top of it.

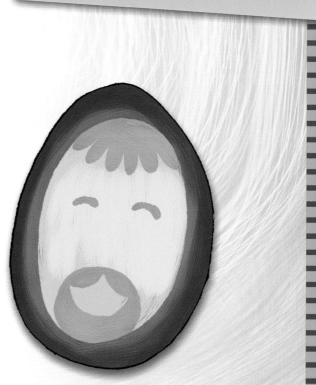

# Final Details

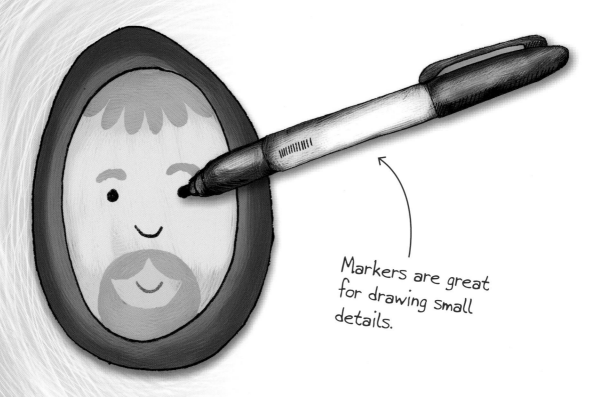

Markers are great for drawing small details.

The last step to rock painting is adding details. A liner brush works well to make small lines. To make dots, you can use a toothpick or the handle end of the paintbrush. Dip it in paint and then onto the rock.

You can also use permanent markers to make a clean edge between colors, to write words, or to add details. Make sure the paint is completely dry before you draw on it with markers.

If your finished rock is going to sit on a table or other piece of furniture, you may want to make sure it won't scratch the surface. Look in the hardware store for small felt circles. Peel off the sticky back and place the felt circle on the bottom of your creation.

If your rock is going to go outside, you may want to seal it to protect it from the weather. Art, hobby, and hardware stores sell varnish. Varnish is a clear coating that you can paint or spray over your work. Even if you seal your rock with varnish, you may still want to take it inside before a wet, snowy winter.

**MESS UP? NO PROBLEM!** If you make a mistake, just paint over it. Or turn your mistake into a new idea. Some of the best art comes from these happy accidents!

Varnish helps seal in the paint.

VARNISH

# Welcome Bouquet Rock

Welcome mats greet visitors at your door. You can make visitors feel welcome with a rock, too! Find a large rock and decorate it with flowers. It will give guests a bright, cheery hello when they come to visit. Indoors, you can use this rock as a doorstop to welcome friends to your room.

## Materials

Large, smooth rock
Pencil
Paints in a variety of colors,
    including green and white
Brushes

Paper
Cotton swab
Permanent markers
    in a variety of colors
Varnish (if desired)

## Steps

1. Use a pencil to draw a line around the rock about a third of the way up from the bottom to define your grass area. Draw a ribbon shape in the top two-thirds where your "welcome" sign will go.
2. Paint the top two-thirds (except for the ribbon area) with a color slightly lighter than your flower color. Let the rock dry.

3. Next, paint the bottom third of the rock green, making grassy lines up in the top color.

4. Fill in the ribbon shape with white paint. Let it dry.

5. With a paper and pencil, sketch your favorite types of flowers. Draw or transfer them onto your rock. Paint in all of the petals with your flower color. Paint the leaves green. Let the paint dry.

6. Use a cotton swab to place dots of paint in the center of each flower. Let the paint dry.

7. Outline all of the flower details with a permanent marker. Add grass lines with a green marker. Outline the ribbon with a black marker.

8. Draw or print out the word WELCOME and transfer it onto the ribbon shape. Or write the letters right onto the rock with a pencil. Retrace them with a marker.

9. If you want to give your rock extra protection, seal it with a coat of varnish.

Greet guests with this cheery welcome.

**19**

# Garden Gnome Stones

Have you ever had a little gnome living in your garden? Look for pointed rocks to make these funny little friends. Hide them among plants in an outdoor garden or among the stems of an indoor potted plant.

## Materials

Small- or medium-size
  rock with a pointed tip
Pencil and paper
Red, pink, brown, white, blue, and yellow paint
Brushes
Black and red permanent markers
Varnish (optional)

## Steps

1. Trace the outline of your rock onto a piece of paper. Sketch out your gnome's details. Transfer or draw the image onto your rock.

2. Paint your gnome's cap, face, beard, shirt, and pants different colors. Paint colors that are not touching each other first (such as his cap, beard, and pants). Let them dry, then go back to paint the other colors (such as his face and shirt).

3. When the paint is dry, outline each part with black permanent marker. Draw in the gnome's belt. Draw a line for his legs, small black shoes, and two dots for eyes.

4. With a red marker, give him a smile.

5. If you want to give your rock extra protection, seal it with a coat of varnish.

GARDEN CRITTERS
Lots of other little creatures live in gardens. Find flat oval rocks to make toads or tiny round rocks to make ladybugs and other beetles to keep your gnome company.

When you are done, place your gnome at home in a garden.

# Rockin' Shoes

Walk this way! Look for shoe-shaped rocks and then design a favorite pair. Place them as a pathway on the ground to lead the way.

## TO MAKE FLIP-FLOPS
### Materials
Flat oval rock
Several colors of paint
Brushes
Permanent marker

### Steps
1. Paint the rock with a base coat. Let it dry.
2. Paint a V shape on one end of the rock as straps.
3. Paint small shapes all over the rest of the base color area. Let the paint dry.
4. Outline the shapes with a permanent marker.

# TO MAKE SNEAKERS

## Materials

Flat oval rock

White, light blue, and dark
blue paint, or other
colors of your choice

Brushes

Blue permanent marker

## Steps

1. Paint the rock with a white base coat.
   Let it dry.

2. Leave the toe area and edges of the
   rock white. Paint the rest light purple
   (or your favorite sneaker color).
   Let it dry.

3. With a darker shade of your color, paint
   a large hole at the top of the sneaker. Then paint two
   lines down from the hole to the toe. Dip the handle of the
   brush in the paint, and make three dots on the sides of
   each line as shoelace holes. Let the paint dry.

4. Outline the large hole, shoelace holes, and lines
   with a permanent marker. Draw a line all
   around the white edge of the shoe, too.

5. Paint laces with the white paint. Let it dry.

# Pebble Pins

Wear these pebbles everywhere you go!

Small, flat pebbles are perfect to wear as jewelry. Think of little images and paint them on the stones. Glue a pin on the back, and you can wear the rocks on your shirt, jacket, or backpack.

## Materials

Small, flat pebbles

Pencil and paper

Paint in a variety of colors

Permanent markers in
   a variety of colors

Glue

Bar pins

## Steps

1. Trace the outlines of your rocks onto a piece of paper. Sketch out small images (such as pets, balls, or ice cream cones) that will fit onto your rocks. Keep the drawings simple. Transfer or draw the images onto your rocks.
2. Paint the background areas or largest areas of the rocks first. Let them dry.
3. Paint the rest of the colors of your images. Let the paint dry between colors, if needed.
4. Add and outline details with permanent markers.
5. Glue bar pins onto the back of each rock. Let the glue dry.

Wait for the glue to dry before you wear your pins.

GAME TIME

You don't have to glue pins on the back of these little pebbles. Find a bunch of similar shaped stones and use them as game pieces. You just need 10 pebbles for tic-tac-toe. Collect 24 stones for a game of checkers. Paint half with one design, and half with another. Find a friend and play a game!

# Speaking Stones

What do your rocks have to say?

Remind yourself or a friend to THINK, DREAM, and SMILE
with these stones that send a message. Or just put one letter
on each stone for **monogrammed** party favors. Mix up a
bunch of letter stones and play a scrambled word game.

## TO MAKE A WORD ROCK

### Materials

Flat smooth rock, any size
Paint in a variety of colors
Brushes
Pencil and paper
Black permanent marker

### Steps

1. If you like the color of the rock as your background, keep it plain. If you want a color background, paint the background with a base coat.
2. Think of the word you would like on your rock. Draw or print out the word on paper. Transfer it onto your rock.
3. If you left your rock unpainted, paint your word with different colors of paint. Allow the rock to dry, then outline the word with permanent marker.
4. If your rock has a base coat, write or trace the word with permanent marker.

Print out a word from the computer in a fun font to transfer to your rock.

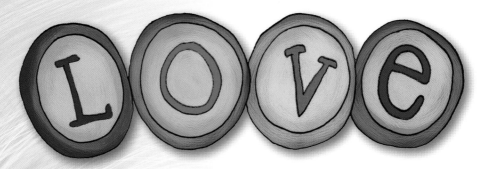

## TO MAKE LETTER ROCKS

### Materials

Small, flat, smooth rocks

Paint in a variety of colors

Brushes

Permanent markers in a variety of colors

Pencil and paper

### Steps

1. Paint the rocks in a variety of base colors. Let them dry.
2. Paint a circle of a color slightly lighter than the base color in the center of each rock. Let them dry.
3. Outline the circle with a permanent marker similar to the base color.
4. Draw or transfer letters onto the rocks.
5. Retrace the letters with the marker that matches your circle outline.

GO FREE!

If you feel comfortable writing directly on the rock without practicing first go for it! You don't always have to transfer letters. But you may want to write the middle letter of the word first in the center of your rock. Then you know how much room you have on either side and you won't run out of room for the rest of the letters.

# Give a Gift

There is no limit to your imagination and no limit to what you can paint on a rock. You can paint the same size rock to look like a tiny ladybug or a huge planet! It's up to you.

The most special gifts you can give are ones you make yourself. Your family might enjoy a rock painted to look like your pet. You can make rocks for an outdoor path in your yard or holiday decorations that everyone can enjoy. Give your friends rocks painted with their names or the names of their hobbies, or even rocks that look like them!

Rocks can be a gift to yourself, too. Do you want to remember a special vacation? Collect rocks while you're there. Then paint them with images from the trip when you get home. Paint rocks with things that make you happy, and place them on your windowsill or on your dresser so you can look at them every day.

Some rocks are even small enough to keep in your pocket. Take them with you wherever you go.

# Glossary

**canvas** (KAN-vuhs) a stretched piece of fabric on which artists paint

**coat** (KOHT) a layer of paint

**erode** (i-RODE) to wear away gradually by natural forces

**font** (FAHNT) a style of type

**humidity** (hyoo-MID-i-tee) the amount of moisture in the air

**minerals** (MIN-ur-uhlz) solid substances found in the earth that do not come from plants or animals

**monogrammed** (MAH-nuh-gramd) made a design from letters, usually someone's initials

**transfer** (TRANS-fur) to move from one place to another

# For More Information

## Books

Fisher, Diana. *Rockin' Crafts: Everything You Need to Become a Rock-Painting Craft Star!* Irvine, CA: Walter Foster, 2009.

Kranz, Linda. *Let's Rock!: Rock Painting for Kids*. Chanhassen, MN: NorthWord Press, 2003.

McCully, Emily Arnold. *The Secret Cave: Discovering Lascaux*. New York: Farrar, Straus and Giroux, 2010.

Mis, Melody S. *Exploring Caves*. New York: PowerKids Press, 2009.

Wellford, Lin. *Painting on Rocks for Kids*. Cincinnati, OH: North Light Books, 2002.

## Web Sites

### Geography4Kids: Rock Types

*www.geography4kids.com/files/earth_rocktypes.html*

Learn about different kinds of rocks and how they form.

### National Gallery of Art: The Art Zone

*www.nga.gov/kids/zone/zone.htm*

Look at artwork to get ideas for your own projects.

### USGS: Schoolyard Geology

*http://education.usgs.gov/lessons/schoolyard*

Check out some other activities you can do with rocks.

# Index

# About the Author

Dana Meachen Rau is the author of more than 300 books for children on many topics, including science, history, cooking, and crafts. She creates, experiments, researches, and writes from her home office in Burlington, Connecticut.